Petals n Pebbles

Harmony of the Soft and the Strong

DESH BIR SHARMA

BLUEROSE PUBLISHERS
India | U.K.

Copyright © Desh Bir Sharma 2024

All rights reserved by author. No part of this publication may be reproduced, stored in a retrieval system or transmitted in any form or by any means, electronic, mechanical, photocopying, recording or otherwise, without the prior permission of the author. Although every precaution has been taken to verify the accuracy of the information contained herein, the publisher assume no responsibility for any errors or omissions. No liability is assumed for damages that may result from the use of information contained within.

BlueRose Publishers takes no responsibility for any damages, losses, or liabilities that may arise from the use or misuse of the information, products, or services provided in this publication.

For permissions requests or inquiries regarding this publication, please contact:

BLUEROSE PUBLISHERS
www.BlueRoseONE.com
info@bluerosepublishers.com
+91 8882 898 898
+4407342408967

ISBN: 978-93-6452-098-0

Cover design: Tahira
Typesetting: Tanya Raj Upadhyay

First Edition: September 2024

Dedicated to my Parents and Family!

Foreword

"A poem is an attempt to look at a highly charged fragment of life with an eye that has a comprehensive vision" says the poet, Deshbir Sharma, a sensitive soul, who has already authored…. Volumes of poetry. Poetry is the preserve of nominated souls, blessed with a special vision by the cosmic forces whose errand the poet is trying to spread to the wide world. The volume in hand has…… 60 plus poems, which represent the world in a kaleidoscopic vision of reality and the romance built around it.

The author is a retired Principal who has always extolled the virtues of honesty and goodness in human character. A sober sensitivity characterizes these poems from the very beginning. Most of the poems comment on human behaviour in the midst of emotional turmoil and the poet comes up with a sage's vision to diffuse complex issues of life and letters when, like the great Buddha, he supports a balanced view of life, eschewing extremes. The very opening poem 'No Conformist' states in clear terms the poet's faith in a multi-polar world in which he declares himself a non-conformist, for he does not adhere to social divisions caused by vicious minds.

In 'White Man's Burden', the poet contrasts the two colours, white man and black robes which stand for justice, but he is in no illusion, for he knows

'Satyamev Jayate' is only an empty slogan. He is very close to what Sheikh Farid, the great Sufi poet says: *Farida, kale mainde kappde, kala mainda ves, Gunhin bhariya main firaan, lok kehn darvesh'* . In exact translation of these lines, the poet says:

> The Black Robes come to my rescue
> As they conceal all my white lies !

'My Shanty Song' takes a dig at our sense of honour at being a free country, when the poor boy does not know what Jai Hind means. "Dreams ...No More' profiles poet's utter disillusionment with the political class, who show empty dreams to garner votes, and then forget all about it. "They were Neighbours" imparts to the volume the partition-sensibility. It is an insightful poem about the mob mentality, and shows when passions are ignited, how neighbours lose their mental balance, and turn cannibalistic:

> *They are boors now,*
> *Because more cannibalistic minds*
> *Persuade and admire them !*
> *They do so because they are men .*
> *And men will , after all , remain men*
> *And behave like self-destroying demons*
> *Because bigger Demons control them!*

'Balance it All' is a serious warning issued by the poet to the world, to stop believing in extremes, and come to terms with irreconcilable opposites, for the sake of the future of humanity:

Learn to balance the extremes !
Or else, things shall burst at the seams!

'Your Own Script' is a scathing attack on the political leadership of the world, who have a forked tongue, and they say what they do not mean and mean what they don't say. The leaders have a special script of their own, which confuses the common man. "Accept it as it comes …' talks of a balanced world view, and a stoic reaction to the happenings in the world, in which men gain and lose as times progress:

Timelines of different editions
Make this mandatory!
And you need neither miss
That which once was!
Nor must you grudge
This one that here and now is !

'Empowered Me' investigates the concept of a woman's progression into an equal gender, but it is only paper work. Externally, she may be dressed well, paid well and respected well, but at home, she has the same timeless mother-in-law whose trite and tough words she has to contend with, that too with self-effacing and self- annihilating humility.

Externals have some new dressing
But that is not the true me!
I am that Brittle , weaker vessel still!

'Cynical Fears'? focuses on the 'bonafides of a poor man', and appears to assert that poverty and goodness cannot be parted. The poor person appears to be making excuses just in order to get some material help from the poet, but when the poet offers him work, the man comes in time. The poem underlines the fact that all the people who ask for your help in the streets are not cheats.

'The Dance of Discord' is a bitter commentary and scathing attack on the bull-fights between the politicians, who defy all norms, and while they gain the reins of power, it is the common man who is considered as a straw-filled buffer:

> *I, the common man, suffer!*
> *They have the bull fight*
> *And I am used*
> *As a straw-filled buffer!*

'My Dilemma' describes the mental condition of an honest officer who is under great stress and grave threat also, from the mighty, who while trying to do justice to his job and to the people who approach him with their problems has to strike a delicate balance:

> *I have to re-assure myself*
> *That I should not lose*
> *The ability*
> *To offer some good*
> *To the common man*
> *Who approaches me*
> *With hope and dreams*

Of a fair treatment!

'My Pantheon' raises an attack on the divisive mentality of our times. The poem in a very simple but sensitive manner asserts that work is the religion of all men who work for the society, and all the shades of work make his Pantheon.

You know who I am.
You know that work is my religion !
All shades of work make my Pantheon !

'As my pledges dissolve', is an interesting and at the same time an intriguing poem, which appears to be making light of a serious issue, of duplicity and hypocrisy which is now ingrained in us, and the poet wants us to forgive each other as God too does not mind our *faux pas* much:

God is the master example of forgiveness
So , He shall forgive my infirmities ,too.
And I can continue to count among good people!
Why do you blame me
When you are guilty of similar slips of conduct?

'In My Take', he almost silently questions how people try to provide rich homes for the stone deities while he believes that deities do not need such lavish expenditure, nor are some days more auspicious than others.

'Be it any land' scolds men for being uniform in hypocrisy and sycophancy of the masters in authority, although the lands differ. 'Live your Expanse' advises man, who has been blessed by God, to show his gratitude for the blessings he is enjoying while his forefathers lived in poverty. 'You know not….' tells the sad story of a work woman, whose husband illtreats her, but she tells him, he does not know what it is to be a woman. 'That is in my own Land' raises a political satire, on how those who are poor [bhayas] gain a national identity only in times of elections, otherwise, they are Bhayas only, whom there is only one thing that defines: tawny skin and dirt laden shirt.

And there is a lot more of the distilled wisdom of a lifetime that lies stored in this holy grail of poetry. The poet has touched major issues of our modern life, and commented on them in his highly balanced tone. Where he needed to be very bitter, he turns sarcastic, because sarcasm cuts more deep when it comes to inflict a serious wound on the psyche of the society. The diction used by the poet is descriptive, and conducive to understanding, while the complexity of thought raises it to great heights of creative felicity.

I wholeheartedly hail this work of highly sensitized poetic creation, which will prove to be a welcome addition to the literary world.

Dr. Jernail Singh Anand
President,
International Academy of Ethics
[ethicsacademy.co.in]
Email: anandjs55@yahoo.com
Laureate Charter of Morava

Internationally translated and published author of 167 books on poetry, stories ,fiction ,non- fiction and an epic titled Lustus - the Prince of Darkness.

From the Author

Poetry comes close to our comprehension of things if it just flows from the page to our heart. If it sounds un-jarring and smoothly and seamlessly conveys the images, perceptions or atmosphere intended to be captured by the poet, it is good poetry. A poem is an attempt to look at a highly charged fragment of life with an eye that has a comprehensive vision. When the phenomenon observed by the poet rides the wings of sensitively chosen words, it charts its way to the reader's psyche and evokes feelings or poses questions or suggests solutions. Just rhymes can construct a song, but may not always be pure poetry which is gossamer stuff.

The present volume is the result of situations , sights and perceptions playing on the strings of a sensibility which chooses not to stay silent, but rather transforms all the vapours of feelings, thoughts ,images and reactions into a cloud , either ethereal or dark , but highly meaningful, nevertheless. These poems are just presentations, and no more! The solutions, possibilities, conclusions or interpretations belong to the reader. They are like dishes carefully carved, but the taste shall belong to the person savouring them!

I make no tall claim. That would be something out of place. I have only tried to convey that which I could not keep to myself. Let me simply wish : "May poetry prevail in every life!"

Desh Bir Sharma
304, Vasant Vihar, Hoshiarpur
Deshbir.304@gmail.com

Table of Contents

No Conformist ! 1
White Man's Burden 3
My Shanty Song 5
Dreams …no more ! 7
They were Neighbours…. 9
Balance it all ! 11
Accept it as it comes ! 12
Empowered 'Me' ! 14
Cynical fears ! 15
Dance of Discord 17
Your Own Script 19
My Dilemma 21
My Pantheon 23
As my pledges dissolve 25
Be it any land… 27
Live your expanse ….. 29
You know not…. 31
That's in my Own Land 33
Born Different, though ! 35
Life's Faces 37
Penury weighs you down the scale 39
The Stub of Childhood 41
Rough patches 43

October …the gentle month	45
Armed to the teeth	47
No right to waste…	49
Ugly Founts of Power	51
Being penniless…	53
Power-lust let loose …	55
Poor , but how … ..?	57
The Beast in Man	59
Nest , Nestlings and the World…!	61
Truth	63
Craft…	65
Pattern in seeming Chaos	67
Emotional Senility	69
Prayers	71
Nothing Linear here !	73
Tell them…	75
I met my God…	77
No Heroes, these !	79
Pleasant Reversals	81
Poems in Colour	83
Transformation	85
Liberator becomes Fetters	87
Midas is sad today !	89
Longing..longing and longing…	91
When Externals matter More …	93
Lord's Bounty Alone !	95

Fighting justified !	97
Good Bye to Ethics	99
Sanctuary of ethics	101
Pangs of Poverty	102
Man and Money	104
The Stamp	106
Cleavages !	108
Two Nations	110
Why…?	112
God in Every Grain	114
Energy	116
Unreal Reality …?	118
Untold Plight !	120
Adam's Legacy	122
Art and Good Governance !	124

No Conformist !

I was not born a conformist,
Nor a rebel.
Was born a Hindu!
Yet wear a steel bracelet
Brought by a Sikh classmate
From the Golden temple
Way back fifty-one years ago.
Always silently say before meals:
"God Thy Kingdom Come !"
Believe in "Love thy neighbor as thyself !"

Have stood against dogma,
Resented sham religiosity,
And yet visited religious places
More for tourism
Than for a focused glimpse
Of the Divine.

Call me a skeptic
Or a heretic!
The truth is
That I have not been
Overawed by the divine energy
Said to be felt
In most renowned places

Of pilgrimage
Across the length and breadth
Of our subcontinent!
I find the Lord
Neither present nor absent there!

Call me what you choose!
I think , I can not afford
To barter this stance
For any '-ism'

White Man's Burden

I honestly carry forward
The White Man's burden
Of assisting the judicial process
But am always clad in Black !

That sets me apart from
The ignoramuses !
I am proud of this legacy
Which some would call
A Colonial Relic !

I am equitable , lawful and everything else
That my vocation warrants me to be .
But I am not sure
Whether I really stand by
The National Tenet-"Satyamev Jayate".

I admit that I do not always
Side with the innocent.
I admit , I do not always issue
Actual receipts for the fee received.

I agree that I talk tall,
But may often fall too low !
I fail to rise above avarice!

I plead the case as cunningly
As I can do !

That is my pitfall
Because everyone needs to be defended.
So I lose my conscience lest I lose my wages.
The symbolic Black Robes come in handy
As they hide all that is seamy.

I take up the case of a known culprit.
I rant hoarse to paint the coal black crime
With white dressings of decency and innocence.
I may fail to stand for justice…

Half of my tribe have no choice !
If they don't do that
They shall starve !
The Black Robes come to my rescue
As they conceal all my white lies !

My Shanty Song

I live in a shanty
That stands on the bed
Of a rivulet by the town
Close to the Dussehra grounds.
The rivulet swells hardly once
In a year.
And when it does so,
We collect our valuables
And hastily wend to the banks
To wait for it to subside.

I know no school
But I know my business.
I sell ball-pens, toys , key rings, balloons,
Candles , Bows n Arrows,
Car shades , dusters n kerchiefs,
And also three-coloured flaglets
Twice in a year !
People say these come
From somewhere called China.

My favourite haunts are city crossings
Where idling cars throb
Waiting for a green signal.
I have but only counted seconds

To clinch the deal!
When accosted customers
Just wave me away,
I simply go giggling
To my fellow vendors
To neutralize the rebuff!

I have never entered a car
Nor a Mall, nor a Hotel, nor a Cinema,
Nor the magic show going on in town.
I don't know why children
With shining faces go to school.
I hear people often say 'Jai Hind'
Will anyone tell me what that means?

Dreams ...no more !

In loud whispers
That resonated across the landscape
And even spilled over to neighbouring climes,
You cast a spell on me !
And sold me a precious dream
....a Utopia which I thought
Could materialize at your bidding.
So I bought the dream
And quietly placed on your palm
The soft petal of my trust!

As feared somewhere
In a remote recess of my mind,
You turned oblivious!
Made my trust just a personal convenience
And brushed aside all my solicitations!
I reconciled and blamed you not,
Believing that you might have your constraints.

However , at your first moment of need
You turned to me
Pleading innocence!
As is my wont---
I forgave and forgot !
Yet again was I shown my place-
As to a lamb which has but only one destination !

Soon you may turn to me once more
But I doubt if I am sure
Whether I shall be outwitted once more!
That gullibility may be a thing of yore!
That may a thing of yore !

They were Neighbours....

They became sworn enemies
Flinging for one another's neck !
Someone had played a game
And they were now pawns
Behaving bestially
Bereft of any fellow feeling
As they were guided by
Animal instinct
Craftily aroused
By the masters whose bidding
They thought was in their best interest.

Men became monsters.
And women became petty creatures-
Fit only to be shamed,
Disrobed and maimed.
And if need be
The poor things became a game
That could be set aflame!
Hapless screams move them not,
Nor inspire awe in their hearts!

They are trigger-happy today!
They boast of might
On the strength of weapons looted

From the state armory !
Someone is there to patronize
Their monstrous affront to the other tribe
As their barbarity is now a pride
Which their backstage Directors
Would often overlook, or only mildly decry.

They are boors now,
Because more cannibalistic minds
Persuade and admire them !
They do so because they are men .
And men will , after all , remain men
And behave like self-destroying demons
Because bigger Demons control them!

Balance it all !

They landed on the moon !
And now, Sun-scan comes soon !
For man of science - a boon !
What to me! I'm just a loon !

Hundred planes hourly shall take off!
And half a billion to build one kilometer
Of Expressway to Financial Capital.
How shall it benefit me ?

Market of branded apparels
Is expanding exponentially !
And textiles shall prosper under PLI
How does it favour us —You and I ?

Studios and salons to shear your hair,
To nourish them on keratin!
To re-bond them , to sculpt them !
But my barber stands under a banyan !

My share is hijacked by others ,
Theoretically , my brothers !
I cast lingering looks
And languish in penury !

Learn to balance the extremes !
Or else, things shall burst at the seams!

Accept it as it comes !

The Journey from status
To commonality ,
From middle age
To the aged peerage
Is a down-hill slide
Full of a sense of slight
That pulsates
In every encounter
With the latest human editions.

A smooth, gradual slipping
Into the limbo of being forgotten
And pushed into the region
Of the not known.
Most familiar faces
Aren't visible on the street !

And those trotting the scene
Don't know you ,
Nor do you know them.
And wonder where is the relevance
Of the vision that you once shared
And stood for ?
Where are people once eager

To talk to you,
And to walk with you ?

Timelines of different editions
Make this mandatory!
And you need neither miss
That which once was!
Nor must you grudge
This one that here and now is !

Empowered 'Me'!

Empowered by education ?
And perhaps , by a job ?
No ,only a semblance, yet !
Taboos stay !
Mother-in-law is still
In her terror image.
Only my burdens have increased!

I have a time table to maintain
Between private and official time.
I have to be a multi-tasker.
Have to do most of my phone-calling
While commuting back home on a scooter
And balance it with traffic hazards!
No choice, really !

I , sometimes jump the traffic lights
Because there is the waiting child,
And the kitchen chores,
And the impatient husband,
And the devouring eyes of the old Mum !
My externals have some new dressing
But that is not the true me!
I am that Brittle , weaker vessel still!

Cynical fears !

Though not more than sixty,
He looked eighty!
Panting even as he spoke
In utterly feeble tones
That sounded like whistles !

As I walked to a Mall
He asked me for some work
As a labourer in a home garden.
May be some tending of flower beds!
Said , his son was in hospital
After a road accident.
And started weeping
To prove the truth of his petition.

I parted with some money
And bade him seek work elsewhere.
Five minutes later while going home
I saw him again walking unsteadily
Towards nowhere!

I waved to him .
Asked him if he really wanted work.
When affirmed, I took him home
And showed him a small stretch

Of grass outside the house
To dig from the roots.
I thought, he might sulk away.

But , no !
He said , he would visit his son
Lying in the ward
And return at eight the next day.
I had cynical fears
And doubts if he would come at all.

And today, he is there!
Exactly on time to prove
That I need not suspect
The bonafides of a poor man !

Dance of Discord

Align by design,
Assume a new name.
And so start the blame game,
And bring the nation to shame !

Accord gives way,
To all pervading discord .
Choosing any excuse,
Or unreasonable reason,
To hurl slander on others.

Forgetting the nation
And its people ..
Abusing and cursing each other
In season or out of season!
To almost brand the others
For maladies that defy definition.

They have a fun time
At the common man's cost!
Gods serve their purpose
To mount to the altar of power!

One almost reigns supreme alone
While the other horde

Has a dozen aspirants
Who wish to make it to the throne!

I , the common man , suffer !
They have the bull fight
And I am used
As a straw-filled buffer!

Either of them shall make it
To the cherished goal
While I shall ever groan
Under the weight of this discord !

Your Own Script

You script your own story—
A fabric of curious weave !
So very disparate by turns.
Of laudable moments of empathy,
And sometimes
Simply of damnable and culpable apathy!

A story of graft accepted,
And of gratification offered!
Of flashes of stoic wisdom,
And of heights of greed !
A tale of victims made,
And of tyrants suffered !
Of roars announcing rage,
And of piety that others envy !

You spin and offer dreams,
And can also rob people's dreams.
You are now an angel of peace,
And now an igniter of clash !
You are a staunch atheist
As you speak about Marx!
Also an exemplary idol worshipper
While you address a devout crowd !

You are the voice for human rights ,
You are the hope of the people !
But when it suits
You also trample all rights
Under your jack boots!
Could you really define
Who you really are ?

My Dilemma

I move to office
And to field areas
In a flag car !
They offer me respect
Which I shockingly lost
But only one hour ago
At the hands of a lout,
Called people's man!

Newspapers complimented me
When I graduated to this service--
The coveted cadre
Called Steel Framework of India!
At the ideal training
They inspired us to become
Flawless creators
Of an ever- new India !

Yet , each day
I have to re-assure myself
That I should not lose
The ability
To offer some good
To the common man
Who approaches me

With hope and dreams
Of a fair treatment!

Still the clout
Of the wealthy and the strong
Poses so many hurdles
Which I have to tide over each day
And each hour
So that I do not
Let down myself
In spite of the weight
Of negatives popping
From every unseen angle!
That is my chosen destiny!
And I am trying to keep it intact!

My Pantheon

I am an Indian--
A Muslim by birth
Living in a ghetto,
A Buddhist
Who came here in 1959 ,
A Hindu
Who holds the Ganges as sacred ,
A Sikh soldier
Offering even his life blood at the borders,
A Parsee
Contributing richly to National wealth,
A tribal
Getting you the best native folk-craft!

Irrespective of my personal deities
I offer my services
To people of all pantheons!
I roll Beedis in dingy rooms,
I put my life in peril
To get you dazzling fireworks.

I go down the gutter
To decongest the sewer lines,
I water the fields before dawn in winter,
I load and unload your trucks,

I break stones
And spread bitumen on roads in June,
I cast lintels for your multi-floors
Though my house may have no doors !

I carve Idols for your temples,
And stitch and embroider attires
For deities and scriptures in your churches.
I weld iron for your grills and gates
At the cost of my vision!
You know who I am.
You know that work is my religion !
All shades of work make my Pantheon !

As my pledges dissolve

I am a literate Indian,
Rather a well educated one!
I publicly declare myself secular
But all my altruistic declarations
Melt and vanish in thin air
When my interests clash with others.
I try to visit all places of worship
Yet lack equality of veneration
If it is not the church of my baptism!

I deplore every fanatic
But at times behave like one.
Even the gods of my religion
Fail to curb my desire
To cheat wherever I can.
I am an honest Indian
But don't mind accepting gifts
Which can facilitate people's official work!

I don't mind taking up cases
To plead in favour of clear offenders of law !
"Who is guilty until convicted?, I tell myself.
I avoid paying the bill when in a group
At the common work place canteen!
I don't mind asking for facilitation money

Before my patient's surgical procedure!
I don't mind sending my research scholar
To do the errands for my wife!
After all , it is only a part of human conduct
Which shouldn't render me less nationalistic !

God is the master example of forgiveness
So , He shall forgive my infirmities ,too.
And I can continue to count among good people!
Why do you blame me
When you are guilty of similar slips of conduct?
It doesn't make me a lesser Indian , I tell myself.
What a relief that my conscience is clear
In spite of all this!
Thank God! Thank God!

Be it any land...

Whichever the continent,
Or the unit called country,
The same tenets of faking
Hold good to serve the masters
To stay in control.
They succeed in their role
When they take their lessons
From Orwell's 'Animal Farm'.

They know that people
At once grab the latest post
And easily forget the earlier edicts.
Rather, people start doubting
Their own abilities to remember.
This is happening abroad
Where an official version
Of falsehood is sent afloat
So that the boss returns to power again.

This has happened in all lands
And in all seasons across history.
It happens in your own land !
Once entrenched, they think
It is their throne forever!

They forget
That time is another name for change!
It must roll on and on
And bring new things and people
To breathe in freshness
Which stands for life!
It happens with men , manners and systems
And will continue to happen
Without the foolish lot learning any lesson
Except that of sticking to authority!
God save such a lot !

Live your expanse .....

Nothing is everlasting here!
Neither status nor riches,
Neither anonymity nor penury.
Your day was waiting to arrive !
You never owned an inch of land!
Only had a poor cottage pitched on stilts
On occupied common land of the village!

Today, in three countries
You have a hearth!
One child in Vancouver ,
Another in Perth !
The village landlord's progeny
Took to drugs
And vanished in ignominy!

The Moving Finger had ordained it
And by it you were dictated
To dream , think and act,
And make your dreams a fact!
Your children read the writing on the wall,
Interpreted Nature's cosmic dance
And grabbed their chance
By invoking education- the great blessing !

The wheel came full circle
And filled the bucket
With material joy
And emotional fulfillment !
Perhaps , in divine scheme
It happens quite often that way.
Thank your often-blamed God
Now that it is Your Day !

You know not....

I lay bricks for your house,
I pull the rickshaw for you,
I pick the junk from your parks,
I parch corn at the corner,
I raise cows for your milk,
I sweep your roads daily,
I scrub and mop your floors,
And do the laundry for you.
I raise fruit and veggies
And rice and wheat, too.

I mend your injured shoes,
And polish them , too.
I wash your utensils at home,
And cups of tea at shops.
Do ironing to smarten your dresses.
I restore the electric supply
Even at the darkest hour.
I lay the table for you
At the Food Court
With the best delicacies.

As a wife, I bear your children,
And rear them, too!
I cook for them,

Fear for them,
Live for them,
And die for them !
You say
That you know it !
Yet, you know not a fraction of it…
Because you haven't
Walked a day in my shoes!

That's in my Own Land

I am either Ram Khilawan or Shiva
Or Bandhan or , may be , Kisna !
The thread that may join
All these names of mine
Is my dress code and skin .

Skin that is not fair,
And a not-very-clean shirt,
As I can't do the washing everyday.
And a lungi and hawai chappals
Earn me the name "Bhaiya"!
Nothing that I may carry
In my heart or head
Is enough to change this branding
Which renders me an alien
In my own country!

Either I don't own any land
Or my holding doesn't yield enough.
So I come in search of work
To another part of my country
Just as they go to Dubai
Or to Canada….
But those are certainly foreign lands …
While my work place is in my own land.

Yet I am a category apart
An alien--- fit to be branded!

The only time
That I feel I am an Indian
Comes when it is election season!
Then in all states,
The candidates come wooing me
With honeyed words
And promises of sops !
Yet I know that it is only for a week or so
And soon I shall regain my previous status ---
An alien in his own India!

Born Different, though !

They say I was born different
But that's none of my doing!
People call it Nature's freak
But, in that ,where is my role !

I try my best ,though,
Yet , they say I am slow!
It is not true , I know!
Ideas do come in a flow:
Only I cannot show
I am as human
As other children around !

People say my grandparents
Blamed my mother for it.
And she would blame me !
Where do I figure
In shaping this
I do not know !

At home ,too
I get more rebuffs
Than embraces or pats !
More beatings than eatings!

Pity me not, Dear Folk !
Only understand me!
Be warm to me!
And love me if you can !

Life's Faces

Religions tell that the same life
Informs every animate being.
Then it should mean that all life,
Whatever its form,
Is linked to all forms as siblings are.

Yet this kinship doesn't always
Find a visible face.
Or else , there wouldn't be
So many countries
And so many governments
And so many clashes
To establish hegemony over others.

There surely are some saintly guides,
Individuals as well as groups,
Leading through noble counsel.
But they are very few,
And their voices often drown
In the clamour for national chauvinism
Putting humanity repeatedly to shame
When the neighbouring country
Suddenly bombards your civilians
For a fault which doesn't lie in them !

Highways have highway-men,
And markets are full of cheats,
Neighbourhood is fraught with jealousy,
Downtowns are known for day light stabbing !
Animals neither cheat nor envy!
They don't kill for sport!
Only hunger can guide them to do so!
But man often puts on some animal face
To bring bad name to the animal kingdom!

Faces behind the actual face can be
Of wolves or foxes or hyenas
Or venomous serpents
Or those of ever-eating pigs
Or of cunning crows
Or docile lambs !
Only very few wear their own real face!
That's the unenviable fate of our race !

Penury weighs you down the scale

Charles Lamb wrote about poor relations :
That was two hundred years ago…
So poverty made people a mote
In the eyes of the rich relatives
Who thought them to be 'a fly in the ointment'
Or 'a frog in their chamber.'

Whether here or in Europe or America…
Poverty is always a curse
Which man can't simply wish away.
It makes you sink to the bottom
Physically, emotionally and socially, too.
It makes you a pariah !
And , by and by, we come to accept it
Or are made to accept it as the divine scheme!

And that generated the silliest division
Here in my holy land .
And they created castes out of a non-issue
And they sowed seeds of acrimony
Simply because some people
By a quirk of fate
Were born poor
And could not mount the ladder of wealth !

Passive acceptance by the afflicted
And callous enforcement by the perpetrators
Made the sufferers go through
Pangs of silent humiliation without protest
And it went on and on….
And that became a stiff tissue
And finally became a festering wound
Creating polarization which leads nowhere
But to greater dislike between the two.

Only financial inclusion shall one day lead
The poor man to a position of esteem
And pull him out of the bottomless pit of caste
To match with advantage
His peers now posing as superiors
Though this superiority
Is only a façade to hide their inability
To appreciate ' Maanas ki jaat , sabhe eke pahichanvo!'

The Stub of Childhood

The stub of childhood in you
Is always looking up for a chance
To peer through time's window
And impinge on your actions,
Thoughts , dreams and speech!
No matter how hard you push it back,
To keep from public view
Simply because you think
That you have grown old
Or perhaps that's how
The world looks upon you.

That child in you is your best part
Never stub it, nor snub it nor rub it !
Only eighties don't bring you
To the proverbial second childhood.
You have been that child…
Even at forty and fifty and sixty!
Only you do not acknowledge it
Since you think you have grown up
And should not look a child.

That is being unfair to yourself.
Let the child in you be adored,
First by you and then by others

Because that's your most likeable version!
At every turn of things,
In a single day,
We revert to our childhood events
Dozens and scores of times
And that defines our life in the present!

Re-live the pranks with playmates,
Remember your acts of mischief at school,
Or having teased your siblings,
Or having bothered your parents
With your carelessness.
And then you will have a pleasant time
With everyone around….
Spouse , friends , children or associates.
Let truth not be nipped !
Your truth lies in your childhood!
Never stub it ! Never snub it !
Let it prevail !

Rough patches

We usually look for
A smooth sailing
And often dread rough patches !
Uncharted paths
Frighten us.
And we opt for the usual
And the comfortable
And allow ourselves
To turn into weaklings!

Unless brought to face a challenge
We remain passive swimmers
Drifting like leaves in a stagnant pool!
A sudden jolt can seem to break you,
But that is just for a moment!
The trauma gets absorbed
And you instantly accept
The fact of the new situation.

The next moment onwards
You start arranging the fallen blocks
To reconstruct from the salvage
As even the darkest event
Is bound to propel you
To rise , brace up and rebuild

Whatever you can,
Out of what you have still left out.

This happens in the vegetable world
Where even traumatic pruning
Of fruit trees leads to better crops.
The tree understands
What is expected of it.
And responds to the situation
And throws up new shoots
With more productive hormones!
The orchard is once again
A thrilling , throbbing green patch
Telling man that Rough patches do lead
To renewed and fuller life !

October ...the gentle month

A comforting bridge
Between sizzling months
And the chilling spell
October comes as a relief
When the scorching sun relents
And its tilted rays
In stead of pricking
Start caressing all things—
Stones , rocks and hills,
And all forms of life…..
Human, animal and plant.

A soothing, cool , temperate wind
Touches your cheeks and arms
Brushes past the leaves of trees
Which now heave a sigh of relief
And glisten in a waxy green hue
With a surface tender as a child's skin.

Its cousin March brings
A similar sense
Of riddance from blood chilling
Cloudy , foggy , frosty days.
An adieu to sweaters and coats
To quilts and to heavy blankets!

Now , in October
We have a maturing sun
That ripens all lime fruit
And pumpkins.
It ushers in the period
Of mustard leaves
The favourite green dish of Punjab!

If an ideal month there could be !
It could either March or October be !

Armed to the teeth

This world is ever armed to the teeth...
Now against neighbouring countries
And now against enemies of allies.
Man has mastered the art to perpetuate
The fighting instinct
Inherited from his jungle days.

Conventional weapons,
And the new age mass-killers
Bedeck the world's ugly arsenals
Making the State Heads
Trigger-happy at the slightest flutter!
Yesterday it was Ukraine,
And now it is Israel !

In fact weapon-happy humans
Can not abandon their armoury
Which can be at times fierce and wild
Though sometimes innocent and mild!

The peacock's dance is a weapon
To disarm the pea-hen.
Tears are the best arms with women!
Screaming comes handy
To the adamant children!

Non-violent protest served Gandhi the best.
While the post-Gandhian world
Is hell bent upon some kind of nuclear test.

Against any kind of hatred
Love is the weapon that serves best !
It can disarm ferocious beasts,
Can convert enemies into companions.
The solution lies not in blasts
But in untainted love that lasts !

To thaw the silence between you and me
Let this verse my weapon be !

No right to waste.....

Man has no right to waste
That which he cannot create…
The red river of life….
The blood that runs through
Every vessel in every human
Makes this life go on….
And can never be produced
Outside the living body!

Then where do we get the right
To shed it out of whim
Because you think it is not 'my blood'?
My blood , your blood , bad blood
Blue blood , Old blood , young blood
Are only linguistic-toying with words
Which don't get us the license
To do things in cold blood
And descend upon another group,
Individual or race
With the iron hand
That knows no human emotion
And revels in killing
Like demons !

That is what nations

And groups , racial, religious or political
Are perpetrating on innocent masses!
Turning the so called rulers
Or Group Leaders
Into Mechanical Retaliators
Vowing to decimate,
Nay annihilate the other.

Peace inducing organizations….
Persuaders in favour of parleys
Are only silent watchers
Feeling helpless and unheard.

Blood soaked battles,
Genocide and words of revenge
Do not announce any human virtue.
It is animal nature!
Let men sit in good counsel
And waste not life, if they cannot create it !

Ugly Founts of Power

Man ever runs after power….
He chases authority
Through money,
Through political leadership
Gained by all means, good or evil!
And through the flaming
Of sectarian sentiments of gullible masses,
Turning youth into easy victims
To spread large scale hatred
Against every other Faith!

It is crafty people who muster power
And then manage to stay entrenched
Safe and secure
While the scalding flames
Radiating from unruly power
Scorch only the unguarded , hapless citizen
Who, in good faith, trusts the mighty
As his savior, well-wisher and protector!

The moneyed man knows no hurdles
His purse can solve all issues.
It can buy any favours.
It can raise financial empires
On the strength of what he has robbed

From the common man's sweat !
His strength is the victim's weakness.
His gain is my loss , your loss…
This, he very well does know
And tries ever to maintain the status quo!

Time and clime do not make any difference !
It is everywhere the same story.
The clergy must keep the followers
Chained in traditional prescriptions
Even in the age of Artificial Intelligence.
That is how they can retain power
Though it does only misery shower !

The Leader knows no kinsmen
While pushing them into strife…
He knows them only while
Cornering benefits, financial or of authority!
They are the ladder to rise to the top.
That is what long ago Machiavelli taught.

Being penniless.......

You can never know
What it means
To have no currency note
Or a coin
Either while you are hungry
Or when you need
A carriage to reach home
Or when you need to pay the doctor
For his services in emergency.

That is an accursed moment!
A pitiable situation!
A deplorable mental state!
An unenviable human equation
In which everyone else seems to have
What you don't !

Whom shall you blame?
Yourself ?
May be , perhaps !
But only if you are a gambler and squanderer !
But , not yourself , if you never had enough
And to spare and fall back upon!

If want is your only destiny

If hunger and scarcity are your only lot
If helplessness has been your share
Then ,really, there is no light there!
Only a man with an empty pocket knows
His privations and his throes!

Either you save your self respect
And decide to suffer and starve
Or take to endless borrowing or begging
Which surely compromises
Your human dignity !
And that's a pity!
And that's a pity !

Power-lust let loose ...

Missiles zoom…
Bombs boom…..
Towers grounded,
Homes made debris,
Death scattered,
Men maimed,
Children charred,
Womanhood compromised!

That is the sight of devastation
Authored by Megalomaniacs
To whom nothing and no one matters
More than their vaulting ego!

History is full of such villains
Yet their tribe
Takes pride
That they still thrive !

What kind of pride is that ?
What do they try to prove ?
What do they gain ?
Whom do they really kill?
Do they know their victims?
Are any scores really settled

By exterminating
The masses
Or paid soldiers
Who are there in uniform
Just because they need means of livelihood?

It takes ages to heal the wounds
Of wars that spell genocide
And mutilate the human race.
They are ugly scars on earth's face
Warlords may earn momentary attention
But they surely walk out of Lord's Grace !

Poor , but how … ..?

Are you poor
In a land of plenty
Where the per capita income
Rises 13.7 % annually ?
National per capita net income
Stands at Rupees 172000.

Which means
That every man's monthly share
Comes close to rupees 14000 !
Does that seem to announce poverty ?
Nay , our statistics can't be wrong !
Then where does it go ?
Why do 19 crore Indians
Go to bed hungry every night?

God knows …..
Our figures are sincere !
May be Google has faltered
In collecting its information.

But then why do people sleep in tents ,
In shacks , in polythene enclosures ,
In thatched huts and under the open sky?
Why do they ask for food

Outside eateries ?
Why do children lick from abandoned plates?
Why do they collect rotten fruit
From near the auction sites
In the fruit market ?

The Ministry says, we don't know !
Our calculations are simply immaculate !
Not the Government's fault
If the Industrialist and the business tycoon
Earn a million times more
They do it legitimately
And their income ,too, does count
While figuring out the per capita income!
Mathematics cannot alter the outcome!
It cannot make the poor rich.
It does its job and leaves things at that !
Why do you malign the governments !
They have done their job ,too.

The Beast in Man

The milk of human kindness
Has turned into the fire of revenge.
Man and humanity have taken a back seat,
Nay , these have been muffled
Or sent into coma!
Or hypnotized by sermons of national honour,
Or by vows taken in the name of religion!

Did people beget children
To offer their youth to the cannon's mouth ?
Were grandchildren brought up
With such fondness and doting
Only to be seen ending up as splintered bodies
Bagged in the morgue?

Merry-making in American
Or British or German or Italian
Or French or Indian Club houses
Goes on as usual
Because God is in His Heaven
And all is well here !

That contrasts callously
With things obtaining in war torn
Lands controlled by jingoists

Who are in love
With their Flag-waving postures
Wherein they ignite the spark of retaliation
And push people into a holocaust !

God of either party to this strife
Has gone into deep sleep
Or has abdicated in favour of the Devil!
Or how else could a seven month old baby
Be bundled as cadaver ?
As she wasn't a party to any clash of EGOS !
She never knew which religion she belonged to!

God stands defeated!
The Beast in man
Has his day!
Alas !

Nest, Nestlings and the World...!

Those who were nestlings once
Have now gone to distant destinations.
They wore their dreams on their wings
And flew in search of fulfillment
Just as we did
Long.. long ago!

They now choose to fly back
Just to touch and refresh…
As may suit their pleasure
Or leisure from the job-routine!
Not to blame, really !
We did the same
When we got these nestlings.
And got less and less time
For flying back to the old nest.

We are used to it.
And sometimes
Longer intrusions
May not be found very pleasant
As we have entered
Upon a new kind of freedom
Which we don't want infringed for long!

Wanderlust now attracts me more
Than staying back!
Longing for being a traveler
Watching and understanding
Men and manners,
People's priorities,
Their hurry or slow pace,
Depending on their outlook and age !
Perhaps the vocation of a Bus driver
Would suit such a wish
As that offers a wide canvas
To comprehend the world of humans
As it boards and travels…
And at the right place and time alights!

It may appear to be an absurd flight!
But that's how the human mind
Sometimes conjures certain things!
These may be fanciful or unfair!
Yet such musings are there !

Truth

Every one knows the truth,
Yet, keeps searching for it,
In nooks where it may never sit !
It is so easy to mark ,
Yet tough to acknowledge!
The politician
And the man of religion
And the man of wealth
And the owner of large tracts of land…
All know what the Truth is!

Yet each one of them pretends,
And publicly sets about a fact finding hunt,
To camouflage his cunning
Lest he be branded
As a thief of people's dreams
Or a usurper of bad intent,
Or a tyrant!

Be it a leader,
Or a Landlord,
Or a trader,
An Industry magnate,
Or a Head Clergy,
A husband ,

A wife,
A child,
A citizen or a public servant…Whoever it be !

All know the truth of ideal human living
In a world of temporary joys
Whether these be Power or Money or Youth,
Or Authority wielded in the name of religion.
Yet , they all remain
Willingly ignorant of the Truth
Which they keep wrapped in enquiries!
That's the escapist's craft
To perpetuate authority
Which may erode
If truth is uncovered
And made known to One and All !
Hence keep it gagged!
Keep it wrapped!
That's the 'Success Mantra' of the day !

Craft....

Craft is so well embellished,
Crude stuff is so nicely polished,
That it passes for elite refinement…
With the simple folk easily taken in
Not only for a ride,
But even for a flight,
To a promised dreamland!

Be these the dreams
Sold by the ruling or aspiring leader,
Or by the Clergy promising the Elysium,
Or the travel offices
Exporting people to job havens,
Or human traffic handlers
Sitting in imposing offices!

All of them know
How to look imposing,
Convincing and impressive,
In their exterior,
And their speech,
And their polite manners,
And assurances of a bright tomorrow!
So that the poor victim
Just bows in awe,

Before he has any suspicions!
But, then it is too late to retract!

That is what happens,
Whenever you are cheated.
Whether it is done
By your own folk,
The nearest of the near,
Or by total strangers…
The truth is that
They know their craft
Of hiding their truth
Behind a dazzling aura!
And that is their Art!

Pattern in seeming Chaos

Behind every event
Human or natural
There is a pattern!
A kind of programming
Behind the visible chaos!

The formula may seem enigmatic
Yet its working is ever unfailing.
The alternating day and night,
The movements of the stars and planets,
The cycle of coming and going
Both of things , situations, phenomena,
Life and its shades
All happen in a pattern well laid out,
Once for all!

Pollination , fruiting , sowing ,germination,
Growth , aging , ripening and fall
Leading to another round of seed-time and so on!
Infancy, toddling , childhood , youth
Age and departure
All come in a sequence
No faltering in the Divine Plan !

Disease does afflict,

And disturb the smooth journey of body!
Sometimes slightly, sometimes grievously !
Sometimes an invited one,
Sometimes in genes received !
The invited one has a cause
And there can be a course
For reversal , if tried
Through the medical science!
Genetic ones have some remedy, too!

Nothing happens without a rationale
Howsoever mysterious !
Loss is fruit of miscalculation!
War is a product of ego,
Ego is a child of undeserved power!
Death is a product of birth
And also a gate to rebirth !
Where is disorder then in the Scheme Divine ?
Surely the incapacity to see is mine and thine!

Emotional Senility

You never admit
That it has crept in.
Yet with passage of years
This child of your fears
Comes to cloud your vision
And creates phantoms like
Suspicions,
Misinterpretations,
Assumed hostility,
Attempts by others to cheat,
Or wrong presentation of things,
Especially by those once very intimate!

Siblings become
Parties to long silences.
Once they never parted
Beyond a few minutes!
And now they avoid each other….
May be , don't want to see each other!
Who is the culprit in this change ?
Only cooling off of our relations by Time –
The Big robber of your joy !

As you and we,
Go past the fifties or sixties

We tend to harden in our attitudes
And lose all sense of tolerance !
Start doubting,
Start fearing,
Start being defensive,
Start accusing others of motives
Which may have no existence at all .

We kill our chances of comfort
And lose the *joie d vivre*
Because we become doubting folks !
In place of discussing
We tend to nurse grudges
Simply because we turn emotionally senile!
This, because we cease to think young
Feel young and take life
As a child takes it !

Prayers ......

It is dusk…and ….
The temples of all religions
Seem to compete….
Each louder than the other
In pleading to the Lord
To accept and acknowledge
The praises
Offered by the paltry being
Called man!

The same repeats every morning ,too
The neighbourhoods buzzing
With blares from mikes.
No matter whether anyone really
Hears and understands
Beyond the simple sense
Of a reminder
That God of one's own conception
Is being complimented!

Do you seek favours
Like a victory or a gain?
Or a Name ?
No , you say
….As you just shy away!

Then why do you do it?
Does your God need it ,
Or demand it ?
Does it enhance His status?
Does He get annoyed
Like the political leader
If not complimented ?
In case , so does He
Then He is no better than you or me !

Nothing Linear here !

Visibly the things might appear,
Moving in a way straight or linear.
Age moving from zero to last year,
Success leaving things in the rear,
Yet the truth finally becomes clear,
That everything moves in a cycle here !

The sky forms or shows up as a dome
The earth , the moon and stars roam
But in a manner that repeats cycles
So do seasons in an earthly year
So does life!

From infancy to buoyant youth,
Then a decline and finally a fall
Into second infancy!
The wheel coming full circle!
Empires rise and then fall !
From a scratch to zenith
And from the zenith to the nadir
That movement sums up all !

From seed to sapling,
To flowering and fruition,
And seed again!

It is a story that spells a cycle!
Leading to another cycle
In the same succession !

Raindrops are round,
So are blood cells,
And the body cells
And the atoms
Having circular shells
In which move the electrons
In a circle!
There is no freedom from circles!
Nothing moves in a straight line here!
Everything is circumscribed here !

Fall and rise,
Rise and fall,
And , perhaps, that's all !

Tell them...

Tell them 'Papa is not at home!'
That is the first silly lesson
We teach our new generation
As it learns the ways of the world .

Then we blame India
As a land of nasty values
And a system that doesn't care
For men and their sentiments !

Keep two types of books--
One for your records
Another for the inspectors,
So advise our tax consultants !

Tell masses that service is your forte !
Dole out free food or blankets
And join the trail of social servants !
Let trust find an anchor in their hearts!

Tell conmen to do everything
To spread the word
That you are clean as fresh snow!
That will seeds of faith sow !

Create a halo of public fame!
Now start your cherished game ,
Assume a slogan-worthy name
And pitch posters of man-size frame!

Tell disciples to fetch more believers
Who could also be shown the door
Opening on heaven and spiritual clarity!
To win people's confidence
Indulge in all kinds of charity !
Then do what you like
With people's numbed wits !

The success lies in telling this…
And doing that !
If you don't want it,
Flap your wings to fly abroad .
This is what our youth are doing !

I met my God....

Being incredibly credulous,
I believe my wakeful dreams ,too!
The other day I met my God..
He was feeling helpless !

I found Him contained
Within the precincts
Of a haloed dome
Cooped up by noisy admirers!

He told me in a whisper:
"I must remain homeless!
My truth is Freedom
From bondage
Because I pervade All…
All that is …
And was….
And will be!"

"These creatures of mine
So fond of glittering
And safe, cozy homes
Have put me in shackles
By raising a home for me!
They are proud of the favour

Which they inanely think
They have done to me!"

I never thought
My God would ever feel
As helpless as that !
Yet, as I said
I am credulous
And almost believe
What my God whispered to me!

No Heroes, these !

No two humans think alike
Then how shall two nations do?
Yet it doesn't any way warrant
Flying at each other's throat!
Still clashes between humans
Or between nations persist
Though they know all clashes end
In unequal compromise
At a human cost no one can make good !

If compromise is the final solution
Then why enact the gory drama
Depriving hapless humans
Of a life of peace and dignity?
No one shall answer it…
As either party devises
Plausible excuses to push the agenda!
Self-deifying is the sole motive
Though every war monger knows
That no one celebrates
A villain hungry of innocent blood.

Leaders across the world use
The facade of democratic structures
To arrogate to themselves the right to kill

Or to sign treaties as they might will!
Governments rise and fall
But the masses live for ever!
For rulers History is the evil mentor
But the Truth of history
Is often missed by them all !

Pleasant Reversals

When you notice a traffic constable
Hold an old woman's finger
And help her cross the busy road…
When you find a noted doctor
Prescribe for you a generic drug…
When you see a cat
Softly patting a young parrot…
When a judge imposes a fine on you
And finding you unable to pay
Offers to pay it from his pocket…
It is a pleasant surprise…
A Reversal of expectations!

When a poor rustic travelling ticketless
Trembling with fear
Is not only exempted by the TTE
But also offered food…
When the stern Headmaster
Instead of pulling up a naughty brat
Admires his qualities in the morning assembly…

When in stead of amassing wealth
A leader gives away even his own estate
To run charity institutions…

When a bus rolling down a gorge
Gets soft-entangled in a tree
And hangs in safety…
It is a sight of relief
And of faith in the scheme of things…
It is a pleasant reversal of expectations !

Poems in Colour

Flowers are God's poems in colour
That entice and fill life's tenor
With a kind of buoyancy…
Even the crudest of us
Get goose bumps in thankfulness !

They always look so inviting,
They thrill and with joy fill,
A feeling of surrender they instill ,
As the scents and hues we imbibe,
With a sense of joy and wonder !

Their right place is
The branch they grow on,
Or the Altar in a Temple.
But followers of Machiavelli
Throw them at their mundane heroes
Reducing Nature's poetry to trash !

The path of the mundane hero
Is paved with petals,
Or his neck is hidden behind
Needled Poems-in -colour,
Hurling gross disregard to Lord's plan.

They are there to spread
The message of smiling
In spite of all things ,
The message of bringing
Brightness and cheer into the world !

These poems never compete
Nor decry the attending thorns.
They offer themselves
To the admiring insects
And butterflies that hover
And hum their love song
In their rainbow-coloured ears!

Kill not these poems
To waste them on humans!
Let them stay as planned
Or let them meet the Lord…
That alone matches their majesty and grace!

Transformation

He was meant for higher things !
Ever since childhood,
He would avidly devour books,
He read the classics,
And exuded wisdom
In every word he spoke!

He studied scriptures,
Not only of his own church,
But of all Faiths , big or small.
His thoughts inspired reverence,
His actions reflected divine bliss,
And people reposed much faith in him!

For best counsel they would flock to him
So… he was learned and holy !
In essence , he was larger than life
In almost everything !
He was invited to speak
From international forums !

It was all so good and ethereal
Till one day Mammon embraced him
And goaded him
To do something big for the nation.

And he chose to be a Parliamentarian ..
His past made it a cake-walk for him !

Now his skills and learning
Came to pay for a speedy harvest !
He amassed money,
Won massive public support,
Spun impossible dreams for the nation,
And made people lobby for his elevation!

Finally, the classics and scriptures
Received a hasty burial !
Untruth became his favoured tool,
Deceit became the best ladder,
And , once again he proved
That he was meant for higher things !

Liberator becomes Fetters

I am given to understand
That Faith in God
Is the only religion .
But which God ?
Mine or thine?

That is the question
Which has fanned
So much fire
Of hatred and violence,
Of death and destruction.

There are so many religions though,
Their own one is the best, people say.
Yet this very knowledge has the seeds
Of all rancor and all carnage
That wraps the world today .

Conversions are a mission!
Breathing out venom
Against other faiths is an agenda!
All that goes in the name…
Of service to one's own God!

Makers and sellers of weapons,

Buyers and users of lethal tools,
All claim to be serving the Lord
Of their own conception .
Yet this is their public image of God.

The actual God they serve
And idolize is Mammon !
It is Satan !
Nor the One Master !
Nor the Son of God !

Religion , the Liberator……
The great Torch-bearer…..
Is twisted and disfigured
And made a means
To put men in fetters !

Midas is sad today !

Every body longs to gain the Midas touch.
But, when I met Midas some years ago
In his new corporeal frame,
He was disenchanted with Gold.

He said: "Days of kings are gone now,
Leaders have voters as their cash-cow,
It is what they call the age of democracy
Where leaders lap up people as a delicacy"

He told that in this age of remote impact
He was longing for a new boon !
His gaze should send people into a swoon
So he wins their hearts by a visual spell !

Soon I learnt that he had won his boon
From the Granter of all human wishes !
He was blessed again and wooed by one and all
Held every citizen in his thrall !

He was everything, he was everywhere !
He was in every heart, his image on every wall!
All obstacles humbled , all adversaries flattened !
He was President Midas..a Happy Midas after all!

Today I met him again after years,
As I saw Him , I hid my fears,
He was again in tears, as he said :
"No challenges left..it doesn't please any more!"

A Midas shall never be happy for long!

Longing..longing and longing....

The Indian deities are said to long
For a human life on the earth
As that is claimed to be the apex rung
Of God's pleasure called Creation !

Here in human life
We have fulfillment
Of longings of senses
Of heart's desires!
There is beauty,
There is luxury,
There is wealth,
There is power.
To long for !

Indian spiritual lore
Encourages a longing
For salvation, too.
A liberation…
From the cycle
Of life and death !

That, if actually possible,
Would be longing for
Non-existence!

Can that ever be
Something worth seeking
As compared to existence ?
Longing is the essence of life ...
Then why spurn life
And work for Non-existence ?

When Externals matter More ....

All wise men believe
That real human material
Lies not in flesh or looks
But in the human mind.

Yet that seems true only
As long as man does not
Lose this sense in the flush
Of money and wealth.

Once into the world
Of plenty and glitter..
He starts embellishing
And polishing the externals.

All this always happens
At the cost of internal worth.
What matters is dresses and shoes
Trendy tops and bottoms!

Majority do assess and get
Assessed through their hair styles,
Perfumes , wraps, coats and purses…
Externals win and the internals yield!

Wardrobes that are proudly stuffed,
Shoe racks that have unused pairs,
Woollen suits that would suffice
Even if the winter were year-long!

Where does this plenty lead to
Except to a kind of vacuum ?
A shallow and hollow life…
That restricts itself to appearances.

Lord's Bounty Alone !

On the Great Ocean Road,
Along the Great Pacific ,
Heading towards Twelve Apostles
Comes the Lorne Beach
Offering a favourite spot
To bathers and sea-surfers !

It is the haunt of week-end revellers
Coming in hordes
Comprising diverse communities
Flocking from all parts of the world.

Carrying loads of provisions
And plenty of ale !
They are here to forget
The fret and fury of the week
And experience a merger
With Nature's celestial elements !

They are aware of only One Lord
Who runs this universe !
They care not to remember
The names of their Prime Ministers
As they dance in tune with
The Great Ministry of the Universe !

Andrew's Chicken Point
And Surfers' Haven
Overlooking the Lorne Beach
Survive in bliss without
The blessings of the political masters !

The only bounty that matters
And lets people stay lively
Is Lord's Bounty alone !

Fighting justified !

Motiveless fighting for fun
Is not a normal human attribute.
It can be our acquired craft
For some cunning gains.
Only small children,
Yet to come out of animal instinct
Can be exempt from this taint.
Not the grown ups !

Yet , fighting for existence is a right !
When the Bull buffalo brought to bay
By a less skilled lion or leopard
Realizes that it is a 'Do or die',
He strains every possible muscle
And uses his horns to full advantage,
Flinging the tyrant predator
To a fatal fall or inglorious flight !

Evil needs be challenged,
Defeated and crushed
And shown its place
As was done in the Ramayana!
At Kurukshetra , the Lord
Advising Arjuna had justified
Confronting the unjust

As a matter of Duty !

Though not a normal human attribute,
Fighting may become a duty
And the only option
To stay in dignified existence.
In that situation , carry no qualms
Of conscience !
Just act like the desperate bull
Flinging the enemy to a crushing defeat !

Good Bye to Ethics

They stand in the hallowed halls….
…Halls of compassion, care and healing!
They got initiated into this trusted tribe
After a sacred Oath to treat the sick
With equanimity, selflessness and concern,
Believing their services are worship !

When they examine the sick people,
They seem to land into the role of God!
Most of them match up to that ideal
And dole out hope, health and well-being!
They prove to be angels of rejuvenation,
And add a sunny brightness to the dark clouds.

Those who betrayed the oath
And chose to be Mammon's men
Become money-suckers
And entice the suffering lot
With promises
Which may be only half-truths!

Such buck-makers take to advertising!
Wall hoardings and radio Ads..
Hold out wonder-results
Even for maladies generally fatal!

They first ask about insurance covers
Or cashless treatment financed by agencies!

In the hands of these deserters of Oath,
In their facade with hidden deep pockets
Where can a patient expect selfless ,
Loving , compassionate healing touch?
First, they rob people of their money
And finally push them down life's edge !
Good bye to ethics ! Goodbye to ethics!

Sanctuary of ethics

Un-haunted by shadows of past sins,
Dwells in brightness a conscience clean,
That cares not for ruffles nor for dins
But enjoys serenity , calm and grace !

A clean conscience is God's own face
It stands no stains of remorse or tactics
It is a haven of cherished human ethics
And a tranquil sea of love and embrace !

It echoes harmony in every stance,
And sings praises for life's upright tenor
It has no time to rue, or regrets to whisper
But only a poem of purity to chant !

When God's Will and human choices
Fall in line and cut out a path clear
Grace and success are always there
Ethics prevail and quell all noises !

A conscience clean is a celestial garden
Where flowers of innocence bloom.
An untarnished sanctuary for virtue
And an unvarnished home for ethics !

Pangs of Poverty

No one ever invites poverty,
Even at birth it comes to sit at one's door
Then it pushes its fangs with alacrity,
Giving men eyes that ever implore !

It brings a spell of hunger and want,
Ushering in a dimness in all dreams.
Makes life just a series of silent screams
And a journey down life's slant.

A tale of hunger and unseen tears,
A trail of disgrace and lurking fears.
A compulsion to stretch your hand
To seek help , money or a favour!

Makes men eat from thrown plates,
Makes life a haunting song,
And a tapestry of endless want,
Where suffering is woven into daily chore.

We look at the poor men..
And say or feel certain things,
But then just pass by!
All such feeling is barren empathy!

Let every human heart feel the ache..
And some resolve make,
To do something instantly,
To share what we easily can !

May no one be born poor !
People only spurn them…
Calling them accursed ones !
But it's not so! It's not so !

Man and Money

Where man and money meet,
They build an altar of deceit,
For ruthless Mammon to seat,
For all records of avarice to beat!

Money stands as a wall,
Between man and man.
The seeker fleeces all
As best as he may or can !

Norms or ethics, man flings,
Of success alone he sings !
All other men are his rivals
Who feel the heat of his lust!

Then man knows no relations :
Siblings are cheated !
Parents are deserted !
Workers are exploited !

He burns in the fire
Of desire for more!
At every lost chance sore,
He looks for more and more !

For such a man
Success means money.
In politics , business or in church,
His be-all is money and money and money!

The Stamp

I like to wear the stamp
Of being a nice, noble man.
The title of being God's own man,
But then, often, have doubts about it.

Temples I don't visit,
The rosary I don't roll !
Yet God is never out of mind
And believe that He has been extra kind!

At a place of pilgrimage,
Visited as a combination,
Of wanderlust and faith ,
I think I don't lack trust in God !

Yet , faced with a heavy crowd
Vying for a glimpse of the Holy Altar,
I don't mind buying a priority chance
By paying a special fee !

How does God take it ?
I don't know !
Yet I justify, I am fair
In my faith !

This is how divinity
And worldliness
Find a soft seam,
In my scheme of things!

Am I a worldly-wise egoist
Claiming to be a devout believer?
I don't know :
I think, I am honest though !

.

Cleavages !

All around, far and wide
I find the mess of cleavages
Based on caste,
Created by complexion,
Ascribed to religion,
Decided by money,
Or ownership of land,
Or by political ideology,
Or self assumed superiority!

You might say 'It's God's Will'.
But the divine scheme never meant it.
Divine hand is implicated
Only by the crafty cranium
Of the dominating lot
Who try to perpetuate
And justify injustice
Authored by society—
The society of self-servers !

Fair and brown people,
Rich or poor folk,
Landlords and tenants,
The rulers and the ruled,
Millionaires and slum-dwellers,

Consumers and farmers,
Are thought of as mutual adversaries---
All inhuman distinctions coined by man!
All these 'duos' are human creation !

We, as a society did it !
We allowed it space to thrive !
Half of us felt benefitted,
And so never thought of fighting it!
Deprivation anywhere
Is an ugly gift from the privileged ones.
Unless we share what we have
Or love the others as ourselves,
We shall remain sub-human !

Two Nations

I know, I do nothing much
That might compare favourably
With the mason's exertions
Or his helper's toil
As they work in the tanning sun of June
Balancing themselves on a risky scaffolding.

Yet my passive earnings
Can easily keep in employment
Half a dozen of them
Each day for a whole month.
Aren't their services undervalued
Simply because they are so many?

Their rickety bicycles always creak
While my cars run ever smooth.
They nibble their dry chapattis
While I frown at the sumptuous servings.
They are mere receivers, with gratitude,
While , I snobbishly make my choices !

Their dream is a roof overhead,
My flight is for more sprawling villas
In so many lavish locations.
That is the difference of our stations!

We live in the same country,
Yet, we surely make two nations !

Why...?

Why am I... ?
Why are you... ?
When you and I join
We make a world .
But why this world ?
Is it God's favourite game?
Just to keep Himself amused like a child?

They say "He is ever uninvolved"
But I ask :
Then why has He
Created a web of involvements
For man and animal and plant
Whereby they try to live
For their kindred ones ?

Here Truth appears a Myth
And Myth is taken for reality !
The material universe holds in thrall
The reality behind ever eludes all.
Youth seems an eternal affair...
And age is feared like the Fall !
What does it avail the Lord after all ?

Perhaps we have created a God

Whose definition suits us !
We try to propitiate Him
And believe that chanting His name
Shall wipe off all bad actions
And take us on the list
Of His loved ones !

We cheat , we sin ,
We browbeat, we win ,
We defeat, we batter
We admire , we flatter !
We build an empire
Parallel to God's paradise !
And then grumble that God is unfair to us !

God in Every Grain

God is the giver of life
To man , beast and flora!
Have you seen God…. ?
Saints and sages
Have spent ages
Yet they can't give a nod.

They evade an answer
And tell that He is everywhere
And He is in everything.

They say: 'Food is God'!
It sustains life
In all living things .

Man forgets about God
When squirming with an empty stomach.
All eatable things prop him
And he needs this sustenance
Each day no end
Till he makes an exit.

The seed contains food
Hidden in the cotyledons
For the un-germinated seedling !

The seedling needs food
Through roots , leaves, water, air and sunlight.
Starve it of this
And we see it withering!

The unborn fish, frog, reptile or bird
Get their food from the yolk
Securely preserved in the egg
By the Unseen Hand!
Providence provides
For all…..
The born ones
And the yet to be born !
There is God in every grain of food !

Energy

Energy is all…. !
The fount as well as the manifestation
Of life in every form.
Growth, movement, death, destruction….
All things are kept in place by Energy !

Energy packed in Water, air and food
Keeps life moving
With a swell !

Uneven lands are turned into plains
Hills give way to human drilling
Bridges get built across the seas
Lands and life of the enemy
Are decimated in minutes,
All because of energy !

It is there in the waters of the river
Breaking its banks and meandering
Beyond its usual course
To spell large scale devastation!
It is there in the still waters
Of a dam that produces hydro power!
It is there in dynamite
That helps build the roads.

It is there in every man-made machine
Or vehicle !

It is there in its most attractive form
In the shining metal and state currency
Which make everything move fast!
When you want growth
You need to have budget for it.
That is Energy in its glimmering form!

Where Force and love for wealth fail
There enters the third form….
The power of the mind
Changes Failure into Success
And sways everything in its fold

This trio of Energy will always hold !
Nothing else shall !

Unreal Reality ...?

And they say:
This world is unreal-
Because it is mere shadow
Of the truth called Reality!

But I do see it
With my eyes,
Hear it with my ears,
Sense it with my nose,
Taste it with my tongue,
And touch it with my hands!
And what is more ....
I comprehend it with my brain!

Yet , you say
It is a myth !
This world is unreal!
What you take for real is not so !

You say : Our tenure here
Is but a shadow show,
Our exit alone is a truth !

I ask : Who runs the shadow show?
Why does He take the trouble

To put up a show of unreality ?

If exit from the tenure of shadows
Is the only reality
Then such a reality
Would be impossible
Without the pageant called life.

Your morose reality of exit
Is only as real
As the brilliant dance of life!
I say: Both are real !
Neither is mock or sham!
It is sheer sophistry
Born but of pedantry !

Untold Plight !

It is their poverty stark,
That casts the darkest night,
And leaves to their plight,
Dreams deferred and turned dark !

Hutments of tin and clay
Announce their shelters night or day!
They carry the weight of generations,
Though proverbial pillars of the nations!

In fields, factories and upcoming Malls,
They endlessly put in their toil.
In the tapestry of their story
They weave threads of struggle and glory !

They too want to move in cars!
They too wish to sit in bars!
They too want to own lands!
They too wish to fly to foreign strands!

They build the neat and shining airports
They keep your neighbourhoods clean !
They crack the nuts that we enjoy,
We have reduced them to nut-crackers!

They roll bidis and cigars,
They shape the fire crackers.
They shape pots from clay,
They milk the cows and stack the hay!

No silver-lining there !
It's an endless tunnel !
Each day is like every other,
In the trickle of life's funnel !

Adam's Legacy

It all began with Adam
When he tasted the fruit
Forbidden by the Fond Father
And fell from His Grace !

Now man calculates
Even while dealing with God!
Mutilated currency finds its way
Into the Hundi as God never uses it.

Coconuts offered at the altar
Travel to the original shops.
Late pilgrims manage priority
Through paid opportunity !

A costlier anointment of Shiva
Through Rudra Abhishek
Is expected to yield
Faster and guaranteed boons !

An open for all
Sumptuous community meal
Seems to open the way
To Lord's kind heart !

So , the descendant
Of Eve and Adam
Has mastered the art
Of surviving in a tough world !

Art and Good Governance !

They say that the earth
Could be a peaceful planet
If all the Presidents and Premiers
Were poets at heart and in practice !

Nero of Rome
Was a poet of his own description
But known more for his Tyranny
And also his extravagance !

So was King James I of England
Who went into history
As an example of autocratic rule
And of religious intolerance !

And what
If such leaders were
Painters at heart !
Would they prove less benevolent?

The world knows Adolf Hitler
As a mass killer.
And he claimed to be a painter
Which all Art schools disapproved !

Winston Churchill was a painter, too
And War Time Prime Minister
Of the United Kingdom...
But that was only to ease his stress !

May be they were exceptions.
Yes, exceptions can be there!
But how costly they prove
Only the subject people know.

Real artists
Poets , Painters, Singers, Musicians…..
Can never author bad governance.
May their tribe for ever thrive !

About the Author

The author, Desh Bir Sharma, a soul dedicated to learning and teaching, served as a college teacher for 33 years for UG and PG classes in English Literature and retired in 2009 as Principal from Government College, Hoshiarpur(Punjab). He was selected to join Central Services on the basis of combined Civil Services exams held by the UPSC in 1977, but chose to stay back in education and he is happy that he made this choice.

Post retirement, he worked as Ombudsman, NREGA for 5 districts of Punjab for four years. That allowed him a close view of the goings-on in the system and of how people are duped by the crooks that abound.

He has contributed nearly 200 creative articles for the Opinion pages of prestigious papers like The Tribune, Deccan Herald, Daily World, Daily Post, Punjab Advance and Kashmir Vision. Watching and contemplating the affairs of fellow humans and predicaments of individuals, societal groups and nations are a passion with him.

When he feels deeply, he is impelled to speak it out.

www.ingramcontent.com/pod-product-compliance
Lightning Source LLC
LaVergne TN
LVHW041608070526
838199LV00052B/3040